WHEN SUICIDE TOUCHES YOUR LIFE

From Hurt to Healing

A guidebook from one who has been there.

DARLENE BROCK

SMART LIVING IN SMALL BITES

TABLE OF CONTENTS

Published in the U.S. by: The Grit and Grace Project
Address: P. O. Box 247
           Estero, FL 33929
Email: info@thegritandgraceproject.org
Web Address: www.gritandgracelife.com
Author: Darlene Brock
Editor: Ashley Johnson
Special Projects Manager: Allison McCormick
Photo credits: All photos courtesy of Shutterstock and Unsplash

This book is written by the author to share her life experience with the sole purpose of providing insight, encouragement, and hope. The information provided in this book is for informational purposes only and is not intended to substitute professional counseling or treatment.

The Grit and Grace Project®
#gritandgracelife

ACKNOWLEDGMENTS

It is without doubt that I could not have accomplished many of the things I have without my husband, Dan. As my business partner, best friend, and the love of my life, he believed in me when I doubted myself. His encouragement and kind, but forceful nudges pushed me forward as I tackled each new venture.

I am incredibly grateful to my daughters, Loren and Chelsea, and my son-in-law, Tommy; they may never know the wisdom and encouragement they have brought to my life. The many conversations with these three have inspired me, given me gems that turn into words, and made my life so much richer.

A thank you to Ashley Johnson, Allison McCormick, and Tess Lopez is hardly enough for what each woman has brought to this book and all the books in this series. The *Smart Living in Small Bites* books would never have seen the light of day without their hard work, brainstorming, and sheer determination.

I can't forget my co-host and co-conspirator in many aspects of *Grit and Grace Life*, Julie Bender. She has inspired, challenged, and made me laugh until I cried. Without her, *This Grit and Grace Life* podcast would not exist.

The Grit and Grace Life website and now the *Smart Living in Small Bites* series would not be what they are without the excellent writers who pour their hearts into every word they write. Their willingness to be vulnerable takes courage. They are some of the strongest women I have ever known.

Finally, and truly most importantly, I could not have found purpose and healing without a relationship with my God and Savior, Jesus Christ. His grace, mercy, and gentleness have led me through not just the loss of my father but many other good and bad days in this life. Surrendering my life to him was the best decision I ever made. He is, without fail, faithful and true.

And thank you, dear reader, for taking this journey with me. I pray my words fill your heart with the comfort of knowing that someone else understands. May you find the healing and hope that brought me out of a very dark time and created a strength in me I never thought possible.

DEAR READER

There are journeys in life that none of us want to walk. Heartaches we probably didn't see coming. Losing someone you care about to suicide is definitely one.

Having taken that journey with the loss of my father, I understand where you are. I also know where you can go and how to get there. Because I did.

It's not easy nor without its own challenges, but I can assure you there is healing to be found.

This book is to help you walk through your hurt and uncertainty as I did mine. Within these pages, you will have an opportunity to write your own story, embrace the mixed emotions that come, and set your own course toward healing.

My hope and prayer is that the memories you have will return sweet and the hope you find will ring true.

Thinking of you as you take this journey,

Darlene

My Story

I knew my father was having a difficult time in life. It was so very unlike this man, whose smile warmed the hearts of perfect strangers, to see that smile so infrequently. But at the age of 50, having left his position as an accountant, he could not find a job in his field. There were challenges he was facing that he kept to himself, and the depth of depression that descended upon him was not fully known to those who loved him. That is until the day my mother found him in the garage having taken his own life. My father had committed suicide.

I was a 23-year-old newlywed living in Nashville, Tennessee when I received the call. This was my daddy. The man who came to my aide when I thought there were monsters under my bed. The man who woke me up each morning for school by whispering through the door, knowing anything loud would make me throw things across the room. The man who forbade me from dating the hippie boys, finally giving up when he returned home from work countless times finding another one in our living room. The man who gave me away at my wedding, believing I had someone who would care for me well.

My husband and I packed, I know not what, then began our journey from Nashville to Northern Indiana late on the night of the phone call. The ink darkness of the night wasn't just in the sky—I felt smothered by it from all sides. Everything was surreal, as if I was living another's life.

We arrived at my parents' home the next day to a building filled with family. The house had been filled that way before with bantering and laughter in every room, but not on this day. As we parked in the drive, my older brother met us at the car. Walking toward one another, he reached out to me to simply hold me in his arms, nothing said, only tears flowed.

As my husband and I walked through the front door I had entered countless times before, my uncles joined us. One on either side of me, as if they were guarding their niece from the hurt they understood I was walking into. An arm was stretched around my shoulder as I walked toward the sofa. I didn't know what I wanted—to find answers, to get details of what happened.

What I really wanted was to go back in time. Looking into their eyes, with half questions on my lips, my tears continued to flow. They sat me down and answered as I found the strength to ask, "How did he do it? Why didn't we know? What was he thinking?"

Truly, the responses didn't really matter, as the questions had no acceptable answers; he was just gone. This didn't have to happen. I didn't even get to tell him goodbye. My new life had just begun, and he would not be part of it. It felt as if someone shot a cannon, and the cannonball had blown right through my core with no way to stitch up the gaping hole.

This Is the Phrase I Clung to in the Hardest Moments

The next three days were a jumble. My emotional pendulums swayed from anger, through emptiness, to grief, and then back again. I barely noticed that the church was packed for the funeral. I heard very little except a phrase that was repeated several times by the pastor, as he spoke kindly of my father, "Don't mistake the man for the moment." I clung to that phrase.

"Don't mistake the man for the moment."

Walking to our cars from the church, we joined the line that slowly made its way to the cemetery. Upon arrival, my mother, older brother, sister-in-law, younger brother, my husband, and I began one of the most difficult walks in my life: from the cars to the designated folding chairs where we would sit to complete the graveside portion of laying my father to rest.

Words were spoken, a final prayer said, and then we sat as friends and family filed by to extend their condolences before returning to their cars. I remember one lady, I'm sure well-intentioned, as she greeted me and exclaimed loudly, "Praise Jesus, he's in heaven now!"

If the casket had not been placed between us and the gaping hole that had been dug, she would have been thrown in there. That was the last thing I wanted to hear. I didn't want my dad in heaven; I wanted him here. I wanted him to open the door as I arrived for Christmas and to fall asleep in the middle of the living room after his Sunday meal.

I wanted him to be the grandfather that would hold my children in his arms.

The hole that was formed in my core that weekend lasted through the entire year. Many nights I would awaken sobbing, my husband would simply hold me, knowing there was nothing he could say that would make a difference. There were days when I wished so desperately that I could pick up the phone and hear his voice. Knowing that would never be true again made me terribly angry.

This Kind of Loss Is Confusing and Long-Lasting, but You Can Heal

Losing someone to suicide carries with it confusion, and almost inevitably condemnation. I should have known. I could have done something. Why didn't he tell us? Did he think we wouldn't understand his hurt? Did he think we couldn't love him through his struggles?

There is a portion of the faith community that believes suicide doesn't allow you to enter into heaven. They believe the choice made at that last moment ensures your entry is barred. Although I know it is not true, I have always wondered what satisfaction one gets from saying that to the family is left behind. I heard it when my heart was torn, and so another layer of sorrow was added to my already paralyzing grief because of their callous disregard of my pain.

Years have passed and the gaping hole has healed. We named our first daughter after my father, Loren. The man he was and the life he lived deserved that honor.

I determined I would never mistake the man for the moment, especially when I had so many other incredible moments to draw from. But, as in all of life's heartbreaks, a scar remains. Yet what I know now is that scars don't hurt, they simply remind, and that is a good thing.

I still miss my daddy, these many years later. I miss his warm smile, his easy laughter. I still feel that there is a missing piece in our family because of the amazing man he was while he was here.

I wish I could share my days, my dreams, and my accomplishments with him. I wish that he could have seen the life I have made. He didn't meet my daughters, but one day he will.

It has been my prayer that I get to introduce them when we all land in that heaven where he now resides. That is my hope, that is where my confidence lies. I will once again see my daddy with that big smile and warm embrace, catching up then. And know that the God who reached out with open arms when my dad chose to leave this world will do the same for me. He will remove all hurt or lingering questions and on that day replace them with pure joy.

"*Grief knits two hearts in closer bonds than happiness ever can; and common sufferings are far stronger links than common joys.*"

–Alphonse de Lamartine

YOUR STORY

Every person's story is nuanced. Yet, we share a common hurt and need. Telling our own story—even if it's just for ourselves to read—is an important step toward hope and healing. Write your story below.

"*There is a sacredness in tears. They are not the mark of weakness, but of power. They speak more eloquently than ten thousand tongues. They are the messengers of overwhelming grief, of deep contrition, and of unspeakable love.*"

—Washington Irving

PROBLEMS TO FACE

No one can prepare you for what follows when you've lost someone to suicide. I think this is true of most life tragedies and challenges. Each has its own set of problems, and some are often unexpected.

With this loss you and I share, the first hurdles are often the practical. Shortly after my father's death, we worked through those created by his loss. First, the financial challenges my mother would face, then the emotional ones. We addressed the area of the home where my father died, then moved furniture in the rest of their home to help my mother be able to live in it until we could create another path.

But for me, the problems I faced were primarily emotional, and they didn't come all at once. I believe that is true for all who have lost someone to suicide.

Looking back at what those were and introducing them to you in this section reminded me how much I hurt and how far I've come. But to start the healing process, we must look at the problems we face.

I have outlined mine and encourage you to do that for yourself, too. Whether you have experienced the ones I faced or others, take the time to read, write, and ponder. Take your time with this process; it's vital to explore fully, and when you do, the next part of your healing journey can begin.

Disbelief

My father was a well-liked man, happy and always hopeful. His easy laugh and ready smile were what I knew of this man I called "Daddy." But even though the laughter had become less frequent and his smile disappeared, I was stunned. If he could make this choice, he was different from the man I knew. Certainly, I heard the news wrong; he could never take his life. This could not be real.

Did your loss not seem real? Has disbelief led your emotions?

Anger

It was so unfair. Why did he do this? I never thought of him as a selfish man, but in this season that was all I could see. I was so very angry. He chose to end his life with no thought of us. He took a coward's way out, disregarding our needs. Or so I thought.

Are you angry too? Do you feel abandoned, left without closure?

Guilt

Could I have done something to stop this? I spoke with him only days before. Did I say the wrong thing? Could I have known what he was thinking? If I had asked more questions, the outcome could have been different. The guilt set in.

Have you been wrestling with guilt? Do you wonder what you could have done?

Why?

I wanted to understand why. There had to be an explanation—a reason. Yes, I knew the work challenges my father was experiencing. He was a 50-year-old man changing jobs. His family felt different, and his marriage was a challenge. But other people have lived through all of those problems without this choice. I just wanted to know why.

Suicide feels so senseless. What questions do you have?

There Are No Words

How do I answer others? Their questions and even their discomfort with the subject made the pain worse. Do I ignore, glibly respond, or start a conversation? I didn't know where to begin. The subject of suicide, it seemed everyone wanted to talk about, and no one wanted to talk about.

Are you finding this hard to talk about?

I recognize you might be experiencing feelings that I have not captured. I have given you space below to write about your emotions and reflect on how they are impacting your life today.

"Give sorrow words; the grief that does not speak whispers the o'er-fraught heart and bids it break."

–William Shakespeare

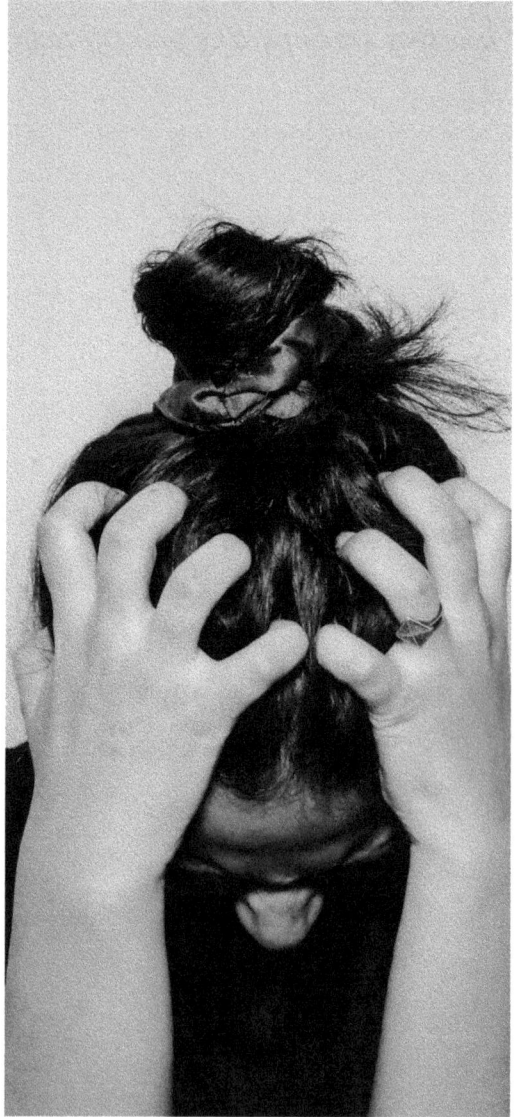

STEPS TO TAKE

The steps you choose to take with the goal of healing are just as necessary as being willing to explore the challenges you have faced. I found they came in different ways at different times. It was never a straight road but waves of answers, emotions, and insights.

For me, the disbelief and anger came quickly. I couldn't walk away from these and move forward in everything else I would face without thoroughly examining and dealing with these two.

The others just snuck in when I least expected.

I found healing in each of the areas I faced. But not just healing; I also found hope, and the ability to bring that hope to others. Sometimes, this seemed impossible, but I assure you it is not.

As I walk through the steps I took, I genuinely believe you can glean a little bit of encouragement in your process as well. If your emotions were the same as mine, please use this book section to consider how I found healing and adjust it for yourself.

If some of the problems you have faced are different, my prayer is the principles I adopted from what I dealt with will help you with yours.

But again, as you work through these and other steps, take your time.

Healing is a process, not a fix. I have provided space for you to reflect on the steps you need to take after I share mine.

I want to leave you with this, a promise that in my weeping, I clung to, "Weeping may last through the night, but joy comes with the morning" (Psalm 30:5, NLT).

The morning may not be tomorrow, may not be next month, but my friend, joy will return.

Disbelief Becomes Understanding

I was in my early 20s. The man I knew growing up always displayed strength, confidence, and joy. His pleasure in this life was unshakeable. A week after he died, I recalled a time when my father and I discussed a different family who had lost someone to suicide.

A girl I knew from high school had just lost an uncle to this heartbreaking act. I was old enough to have this conversation, so we did. At the time, my father concluded, "I don't know how someone could feel so hopeless they would take their own life."

I know he meant that on the day he made that statement. The fact that he ever said this made it impossible to think he would do the same. My view of him at that time was from a daughter's perspective. I was not yet an equal who understood everyone experiences hurt, heartache, and disappointment—even my father.

In the year leading up to his death, he had left a difficult job, my elder brother and I were grown, he felt distanced from my younger brother, and he was married to my mother. He loved her, but she was not a very sympathetic woman in any area of life. My goal in sharing this is not to place blame, but to acknowledge his reality in order to grasp the challenges he faced. We all must look behind the surface. Hindsight tells the real story, the one where joy turns to despair. I only had to look.

Some circumstances in a person's life can lead them to believe that ending it is the only option. Both external and internal battles skew their thoughts, changing their reality. Depression becomes their bedfellow, and suicide, to them as it was to my father, is the way out. Before that depression set in, he certainly never thought this would be a step he would take.

Realizing that life circumstances can affect any of us in this way may not ease the pain for the ones left behind, but it helps the healing. Understanding replaces disbelief, and that enables us to accept that the one we love is no different from us. Hurt, disappointment, and pain will touch us all. When I realized my father was just another human trying to navigate this life, I understood that the path for him became too much.

There is something that all who are touched by suicide need to accept. Life circumstances can lead any of us to make choices we may have never thought possible. There are many things we may proclaim to never be capable of doing only to find ourselves in situations that seem to change everything. Life becomes too hard; the situation feels too impossible.

For my father, it was one day in his life, and on that day, he saw no other way than to make this decision—a day I wish had ended differently. But the totality of the life lived is what I know. My father was more than that day. His hurt was real, but so was every other part of his life. I learned to understand and accept the whole man. His joy. His smile. His laughter. His hurt. His depression. His hopelessness. His compassion. His care. By doing so, I could embrace the treasure of all of who he was, put aside my disbelief, and move toward acceptance, which is a step in the healing journey. You can, too.

Are you struggling with understanding? Are there steps I took that might help you?

Anger Becomes Compassion

Letting go of my anger was a hard one. It felt like my father had decided to leave us when he knew we needed him. He must have known there was so much life ahead. I had just married and wanted him to be part of my future.

When I was alone preparing for his funeral, I stopped getting ready and just started pacing. I needed to unload all I was feeling. I began by telling my father how angry I was, verbalizing every emotion I possessed. As I walked the room, getting more and more vocal, I wanted him to know that what he did wasn't right. I wanted him to know how mad I was that he made this choice. It wasn't fair that we —no, that I—was left to pick up the pieces. They weren't my choosing, and now the pieces felt like all I had left of this man I loved. Broken pieces, and a broken heart.

The emotions you're left with after you've lost someone to suicide take a long time to work through. They come in waves, sometimes waning, sometimes returning. Or, you're hit by another you hadn't even seen coming. This one for me took months. When my disbelief turned to understanding, my anger began to turn to compassion. But it didn't come quickly; I couldn't do that alone. Neither can you.

Those left behind need to find answers to all their emotions, often by searching for others who have lost someone as they have. I spent a lot of time reading and researching personal and research-based accounts. I was trying to understand his rationalization. Was there a perspective I needed to relieve the anger I was holding?

What I learned was this: My father didn't take his life because he wanted a way out. Many studies reveal this truth, "Researchers believe that some people who end their own lives do not actually want to die but feel there is no other option to relieve them of their pain."[1] They want to stop hurting. He wanted a way to rid himself of his unbearable pain.

My father didn't take his life because he was selfish; quite the contrary. In the account of several suicide survivors, they genuinely believe in that moment that those left behind would be better off if they weren't there. They thought what they were struggling with was too much, not just for them but for their family as well.

On the day that he left his precious items on the dresser to walk the path to his death, he thought this act was a relief not only to him but to us, those he loved. Yes, he wanted to end the pain, the depression, the hurt he was experiencing. But I believe he thought his act was ending the pain for us, too, not realizing it would make us hurt more.

That knowledge made me not only understand a bit more but love him more as well.

Have you tried to look through the lens of the one you lost? If so, what did you see?

_____

_____

_____

_____

_____

_____

_____

_____

_____

_____

_____

_____

_____

Guilt Becomes Action

I spoke to my father a mere 10 days before he took his life. I knew he was struggling. He cried on the call, talking about the hurts he was experiencing and doubts about himself and his future. My father was a loving, sensitive man, so tears were not foreign to him. I did my best as a 23-year-old woman to encourage him and tell him how much I loved him; then, we ended our call.

But the day he died, I wondered why I hadn't done more. Even though I lived 400 miles from him, I could have made the trip or a phone call and alerted someone. Why didn't I see how low he had become and step in? To do something. Anything. "If only I had" became a phrase I repeated for months after.

Was I or any of his family or friends guilty, complicit in his death? I can tell you the answer is no. If you are feeling that, the answer is no. Unequivocally no.

I didn't know what depression and suicide looked like. Before this moment, I only had distant exposure; it was merely a topic of conversation. What I did learn is the choice made came from a mentally unhealthy state. Depression, substance abuse, and other mental health challenges frequently lead to one taking one's life. At that time, it was beyond me to understand that.

I also knew he would never want me to carry that regret in this life. The father I knew did love me and wanted the best for my life, including leaving guilt behind.

I could not have known the depth of his hurt; he only shared the surface. You can't either. Hindsight brings understanding, and it also brings opportunity.

As you heal, you will learn more. The knowledge you gain can and will help others: those who may be struggling with depression and those who have lost someone as you have. This became personal to me when attending a convention two years after my father's death. It was held each year for those within the music industry. These events were always filled with the "Have you heard?" conversations. This particular year there was the "Have you heard Bob's father committed suicide?" dialogue. Bob was a sales rep I only knew through events like this. But that didn't deter me.

I looked across the convention floor, spotting him two aisles away. Beelining his way, I grabbed him by the arm stating, "I heard your father took his life, so did mine." His expression went from complete astonishment that I would be so bold as to attack him, to recognition that we were unwilling members of the same club.

We stepped aside to a quiet place where he poured his heart out. I listened as he talked. There wasn't a grand revelation or profound counseling given that day, merely one heart shared with another. I was able to be a sounding board because I understood his hurt. It was the same pain as mine.

Assisting those who are living this loss becomes part of our healing. So remove the guilt and replace it with action. Become the personal story that helps others as they live theirs. What you know and have learned through your loss may become a lifeline for someone else.

Have you found a way to replace guilt, perhaps by helping someone else through their loss or recognizing signs of depression in another's life?

"Why?" Becomes Peace

I wanted an answer. Maybe so I could help others. More likely, I felt I needed to know. Why did my father take this step? I needed to understand what drove an individual to take his life. Yes, I had come to realize he was suffering from depression, and the circumstances that surrounded him felt daunting, overwhelming, and even hopeless.

But others have faced the same challenges and didn't make this choice. They found a way through. Why didn't he?

One factor I had to consider is that he was not the only member of his family who chose to end his life. He had a brother who did as well. So, could biology play a role? As I read more about this subject, research says that could be true. But it also stated that may not be the case. He had four other siblings who did not make the same choice.

I could accept that he thought we would be better off without him. But that wasn't enough to answer my "why." When the thoughts my dad had went through the minds of others, they worked through their depression.

It's years later, and I will tell you this: I don't know why. Not the real "why" that was at work in my father's life that day. I will never (nor will you) understand everything that was in his mind at that time. Why didn't he make a different choice? Struggle as I may, I will only find some of the answers. Not all.

I had to learn that the "why" changed nothing; he was gone, which led me to make a choice. Accept and find peace or keep asking the questions. For me to move on from this loss, peace is what I needed. Peace is what you need.

Healing comes with surrender. Letting go. I trusted the God I serve with having the answers I didn't because he sees every heart. He saw my father's heart every day of his life, even the day of his death.

He sees mine as well. He knows my questions. He assures me he has the answers even if I don't. I decided to accept and seek the peace I knew could be mine. I decided to trust the only one who knows us intimately and loves us dearly.

So, leave the questions you can't answer, leave them behind to move forward. As hard as this may be, it is the only way you can and will find peace.

How has your questioning become peace? If it hasn't, how can you pursue it?

My Words Become Sure

Awkwardness doesn't begin to address the conversations some sought and others avoided surrounding the loss of my father. Some wanted details of how it happened. At first, I felt obligated to share those, but it wasn't long before I didn't.

How it happened wasn't anyone's business. While natural to humanity, the curiosity served only to open a wound, to see my father in my mind's eye in a way I never wanted to envision. So, I quit sharing the details. Instead, my answer became, "It is only the sweet memories I have of my father I want to treasure and discuss. I'm sure that's true of you, too." And I moved on.

Then there were those who didn't know what to say. They stumbled, started sentences, and tried to pretend he died in any manner except suicide. That really didn't help either. After some healing on my part, I chose to step in to ease their discomfort. It was these folks to whom I said, "It is okay. My father took his life, and that isn't easy to reckon with. But it is all of his life, not simply that day, that I invite you to celebrate with me." And often, they did.

Then, the treasured ones who said very little. They threw their arms around me and held me as I sobbed, offering words that only included, "I'm so sorry" and "I love you." Those few precious family members and dear friends received the bulk of my words. At those moments, you don't need an expert, you don't need opinions on the subject of suicide, you simply need a loving and open heart.

It was the trusted ones that I could speak everything to—my anger, guilt, confusion, and hurt. When I did, they didn't offer pat answers or platitudes. They listened and loved. When you find those who can be that for you, and you will, let them in.

The gift they offer is to let you work through as much as you need to, at your own pace. They will walk with you and listen to every emotion you have until your words become sure and your heart slowly heals.

Are you reticent to speak of your loss and how do you change that?

"Grief and joy can co-exist at the same time, sometimes in the same breath—in the same moment."

—twloha.com

FINDING HOPE

My father took his life at the end of September. It felt like mere days had passed since we walked from his graveside, and now we were facing the upcoming holidays. These were memorable times as we gathered to share life as a family and extended family. We were good at the celebration and loved being together to laugh, cajole, and debate, each year making the effort to put aside family drama to enjoy one another. Daddy was always at the heart of those special days, his laugh easy, his leveling personality present, his pleasure in these celebrations palpable.

But he wasn't there. Not only wasn't he there, but it was his choice not to be. Loss by suicide has a grief unto itself. And it was excruciatingly evident during that first holiday season.

The first thing we had to do was find a way to adjust to his absence in the holidays we were facing. This was the first season without him, and we couldn't expect not to grieve, but we didn't want grief to fill our time together. It was too fresh to do anything other than the traditions we had created in years gone by. Keeping some traditions and adding new ones was necessary in the coming years, but we needed a place to start.

It was this year, during this heartbreak, that I came to understand grief and joy walk hand in hand.

It was important to celebrate our faith, enjoy our family, and allow each of us to process our loss. As you heal, you should never feel guilty or confused about the joy that still is part of your life. In the same way you allow yourself to experience grief, you must let yourself celebrate joy. Whether hugging a new baby or sharing moments of laughter, there are always things to be grateful for and take pleasure in. And you must.

Allowing yourself to grieve is imperative as well. When you've lost someone to suicide, it feels like you are alone. It's a conversation most people don't want to have; it's just too hard. But unfortunately, you are not alone. Statistics from NIMH tell us that suicide is the 10th leading cause of death in the U.S.[2] Multiply those deaths by the ones left behind. You are in a club no one wants to join, but there are more like you than you know.

Learning you don't need to be afraid to talk about your loss is a starting place in processing all the emotions and challenges faced. There will be some who are uncomfortable. Others are curious. But you will be surprised to discover the many who have experienced this same loss. Be willing to be vulnerable because you will gain understanding through invaluable shared experiences when you open those conversations.

Sharing your grief is also a crucial part of the healing process. But when you do, I would suggest a few things. You will find others are grieving the same loss as you, but their shared grief hurts you more than helps. My mother was that for me. Her hurt was so real, and I cannot imagine the depth of her pain.

But she constantly wanted to revisit the details of how he died; I did not. She needed to work through her anger toward him and her hurt by listing all his imperfections and shortcomings. It was too much for me to bear. It was understandable, but I often had to remove myself from those conversations.

She and I found ways to grieve together, but I also knew the boundaries I had to put in place for my emotional health. There is a balance between sharing grief and understanding when that sharing is taking you down a path that is unhealthy. Listen, love, and sometimes walk away.

I was fortunate to have my husband of only a few months walk through this with me. He didn't know my Daddy well, but my father trusted him with his only daughter, which he took as both assurance and responsibility. He was my rock. Find yours.

A few friends, not touched by a loss like this, loved me well. They allowed me to talk—to share my hurt, memories, confusion, and tears. They were a safe place. They didn't judge; they didn't offer opinions or platitudes; they listened. That was so important to my healing. It would be best if you found those people in your life as well.

Finally, cling to treasured memories of the one you lost. Don't allow anyone to diminish those. You are grieving because of what they meant to you. You feel the loss because of their impact on your life. Painful reminders surface because they come from sweet memories.

Don't run from those moments. They will not only sustain you, but they will grow larger as your grief becomes less.

But what sustained my heart and walked beside me in each stage of healing was my faith. I serve a God of hope and redemption. One who loves us at our highest point and loves us no less at our lowest. One of his many promises about who Jesus is and what he will do embedded itself in my broken heart. "Through the tender mercy of our God, with which the Dayspring from on high has visited us; To give light to those who sit in darkness and the shadow of death, To guide our feet into the way of peace." (Luke 1:78-79, KJV)

When I felt my grief would never end, I turned to these: "He heals the brokenhearted and binds up their wounds." (Psalm 147:3, NLT) and, "Then Jesus said, 'Come to me, all of you who are weary and carry heavy burdens, and I will give you rest. Take my yoke upon you. Let me teach you because I am humble and gentle at heart, and you will find rest for your souls." (Matthew 11:28-29, NLT) And I discovered these words to be true.

These verses and more were a part of my healing, but I also pondered my father's faith. Would I see him again? I believed so, and I found several sources that brought me hope. However, there was another opinion from some who shared my faith that only drug my heart more deeply into despair. It was unfathomable to me that someone wrote an entire book on the consequences of suicide, including eternal rejection by God. It appeared they felt it was their duty to share what they believed.

To offer grace to those who wrote this, I assume their intent was to deter those who were considering suicide. But for me, it was simply cruel.

My faith has never been afraid of seeking truth, even though I may fear the answers. Even when I wasn't entirely sure of the outcome, I could feel no different at this juncture in my life.

I began by reading a bit from those who held this stance. Some faiths define suicide as a mortal sin, one which cannot be forgiven. They sincerely believe this to be true. As I read this view, it was not without me violently tossing the book across the floor in utter frustration and anger. Yet, I still wanted to know why they believed as they did.

Their premise was created using this verse in the Bible, Exodus 20:13, "You shall not murder." They applied this verse to the killing of another but also felt it was the same for one taking one's own life. In addition to that commandment, this scripture is used as well: Genesis 9:5, "For your lifeblood too, I will require a reckoning."

As you spend time in the Bible, there are more verses that speak to our eternal destination, and they can be applied to other life choices beyond suicide. Matthew 5:22 says that anyone angry with their brother is in danger of eternal punishment. So, if the stance taken is that taking your own life is not within the grace of God, then anger is not either.

The Bible should always be understood in its entirety. When verses are pulled to justify or confirm a belief rather than taken in the entire context of scripture, those beliefs often land on shaky ground.

They are also damaging, leaving no room for the entire gospel of Jesus, who endured God's full punishment for all sins of anyone who believes.

If God's grace is real (and I am confident it is), there is nothing beyond his ability to understand, offer compassion, and ultimately redeem.

Here's what I know to be accurate: I have lived through my sins and failures. "And I am convinced that nothing can ever separate us from God's love. Neither death nor life, neither angels nor demons, neither our fears for today nor our worries about tomorrow—not even the powers of hell can separate us from God's love. No power in the sky above or in the earth below—indeed, nothing in all creation will ever be able to separate us from the love of God that is revealed in Christ Jesus our Lord." (Romans 8:38-39, NLT)

I clung to these words in my relationship with a God who has mercy for me and my father. He can see us through every hurt and heartache and bring us hope. I love what was written in 2 Corinthians 12:9 by a follower of Christ, Paul, whom I consider a pillar of our faith, "Each time, my grace is all you need. My power works best in weakness."

We aren't weak once or twice in our lives; we don't need grace occasionally. We need it each day. I do; my father did. It is given every time we needed it. I know my father's faith was as real as his pain. I am without doubt that he was welcomed into heaven because of that faith, not denied because of his final act.

You may not know if the one you lost held faith in Christ. But I want to remind you of this: when Jesus hung on the cross, there were two other men crucified with him. Both made a declaration, and only one a request. Luke 23:39-43 says, "One of the criminals hanging beside him scoffed, 'So you're the Messiah, are you? Prove it by saving yourself— and us, too, while you're at it!' But the other criminal protested, 'Don't you fear God even when you have been sentenced to die? We deserve to die for our crimes, but this man hasn't done anything wrong.' Then he said, 'Jesus, remember me when you come into your Kingdom.'

And Jesus replied, 'I assure you, today you will be with me in paradise.'"

At the very end, this man saw his need, recognized his sin, and sought the one who offered him forgiveness. And Jesus did.

We don't know the final moments of anyone's life, and you do not know your loved one's final moments. I know God can and has touched hearts simply minutes before their last breath. I encourage you to hold to the hope that he touched the life of the one you loved as well.

You may be at an uncertain place in your faith or need encouragement in your relationship with Christ; if that is true, head to the last section of this book. You can find what I have discovered and clung to in the best and worst of times there. Whether your faith is beginning, battered, or building, we know you will find hope. I have.

No matter where you are in your faith journey, this is my prayer for you, "The Lord bless you and keep you; the Lord make his face shine on you and be gracious to you; the Lord turn his face toward you and give you peace." (Numbers 6:24-26, NIV)

Life is indeed hard, my friend; you know that by what you're walking through today. What you are experiencing is devastating. But hope is real and best found in the hope of our faith. For you, the one you lost, and those who are grieving alongside you. I am confident that hope will be yours as time moves forward.

FINDING YOUR HOPE

On the lines below, take inventory of any areas where your faith feels weak and record any opportunities you see for growth. Consider writing a prayer to God for his help, perspective, and strength.

"*Earth has no sorrow that heaven cannot heal.*"

–Thomas Moore

WHEN MEMORIES RETURN

Life moved on from the loss of my father. Ten years passed since the day I received the call. My husband and I had moved three times— each one created a significant life change. We celebrated the birth of our two daughters, adding the title of "parents" to our list. We had purchased a home, sold that home, and built another. We launched two businesses; I traveled extensively with the artists I managed, and I lived all my life to its fullest.

But that Father's Day, standing in the card aisle with my cart partially loaded, I was caught completely off guard. I was in search of a card for my father-in-law, something I had done yearly for the last ten years. Tears started forming, then ran down my face. I wondered what was wrong with me. I couldn't quit crying. I realized I wanted to purchase a card for my father. I wanted to travel to see him and hand it to him in person. But this day, this purchase reminded me that wasn't possible.

There was nothing I could do to make the tears stop, so I abandoned my cart where it was. I walked quickly to the parking lot, sliding into the driver's seat to let go of all the unexpected emotions. Fortunately, I was shopping alone during lunch hour when the floodgates broke.

It seemed impossible that I could grieve this heavily after all the time that had passed.

After a decade of buying these cards, why did this one hit me so differently? The first Father's Day after I lost Daddy, I had shed an abundance of tears. The second, I struggled. The third, a bit easier. Since then, my emotions seemed to have leveled.

My father-in-law meant the world to me. For seven Father's Days, I had only delighted in purchasing a card that showed him how much he meant. He had stepped in, not as my father, but as a man who loved me well and wanted to be whatever I needed after my loss.

So, why? Why was this year so very intense? Why now?

Not expecting a wound to open again this profoundly, I realized I needed to step back. I needed to look at my hurt, not dismiss it. I had to acknowledge it was no less genuine on this day than it was on the day I lost Daddy. And I had to address it before I could move on.

So, I did. I allowed myself to feel another level of loss, and I went in search of another level of healing.

No loss is one-and-done. Yes, we find healing, hope, and happiness again. We fill our lives with new relationships, opportunities, and experiences—as it should be. We can and must recognize the forward movement in our healing but remember that the hurt can flood back unexpectedly, and it will. The loss raises its head again and stares us in the face, leaving us on unsteady ground once more.

That is as it should be, and we need to expect it. There are layers to life's hurt.

Whether from suicide, anxiety, infertility, self-worth, or divorce, the pain we experience will come back. Often differently, usually unexpectedly.

When that happens, don't dismiss or ignore it. Allow the next season of healing to take place in your life. When the wave hits you again, talk to someone. Reread this book and walk through the journey again. If need be, find another source to help you through this season.

When these waves happen, the encouraging thing is that where you were is not where you are now. Your hurt is different. You are so much wiser, with compassion and understanding you didn't have before. You have healed, but it isn't over yet. Remember that each wave that hits will make you stronger than before.

These seasons are a necessary part of the healing process in life's challenges. The day the floodgates opened for me, I had to leave that cart in the aisle. I needed to shed those tears to find a fresh layer of healing. And I did. You will, too.

"*Grieving is a necessary passage and a difficult transition to finally letting go of sorrow - it is not a permanent rest stop.*"

—Dodinsky

BEFORE YOU GO

Reliving the loss of my father as I penned these words surprised me. I felt a lot of emotions: some hurt, sadness, and empathy for you who are walking through it now. But above all, I missed my father. That is because I am at a place where the memories I hold are dear. His easy laugh rang in my head, the wisdom he imparted was brought back to mind, and his ability to make a stranger into a friend in a matter of minutes became fresh once again—those are the things I hold in my heart.

I am telling you this because you will one day find yourself at this place, too. Where the hurt has been tempered and the treasured memories dear. You will be able to chat about the one who is gone with laughter and joy. You will boldly speak of them with confidence in who they were, not what they did. And you will delight in being able to do so.

This probably isn't today and may not be soon, but, my friend, with complete confidence I can tell you it will come.

Allow time, resources, friends, and counselors to take you on the journey toward healing. The hurt is real, but I promise you the hope is as well.

May the Lord's face indeed shine on you. I know he wants to be present with you every step of the way. So please, dear one, let him.

Sincerely yours, and truly his,

Darlene

THE HOPE
WE'VE FOUND

This guidebook is a reminder that every woman's life is a journey. Every one of us will face good times and hard times. We all have stories that we love to tell and stories that still hurt to remember. While our human experiences may have similarities, there is no one who truly understands what you have been through and who you are better than Jesus. And he wants to invite you further into another journey—a faith journey—with him.

If you are searching and encountering him for the first time, we trust you will meet the Savior who gave all through the most difficult times because he had his love set on you. If you already know him and are building your relationship with him, we believe he will sustain you. If you have felt disheartened by the despair life can bring, we want you to know that God is not disappointed in your doubts or struggles—but is only more drawn to you in his tender mercy.

No matter where you are in your faith, God wants to meet you there. To be your hope and help. And we want you to know that he truly will.

Heather Jonsson, one of the Grit and Grace Life team writers, has unpacked each step of our faith journey: beginning faith, battered faith, and building faith. They are all a part of the faith journey the writers at Grit and Grace Life are on.

We hope that her written invitations will help you join us on this path that leads to a sense of purpose in this life and holds promise for the one to come.

Also, if you enjoy Heather's writing, we encourage you to find more of her personal work at www.heatherjjonsson.com.

BEGINNING FAITH

I wish you were sitting with me today, here in my living room. Here where the gentle spring winds play with my blue curtains, and the warm sun is melting away the frost of winter. There is a shift in the air.

You and I would take a walk, shedding our coats to allow the sun to kiss our skin. And we would sit outside on the patio, charmed by the green shoots pushing their way through the cold earth, which just last week was blanketed in snow. And I would look in your eyes and tell you, this awakening to life we feel, when what was dead begins to awaken, this is what has happened to my soul as I have come to know Jesus.

Have you ever had a friend who, just by spending an afternoon with them, makes you a better person—happy, full, content? So it is with Jesus. He loves you with an unstoppable, unchanging, perfect love, and his love changes you. This is the beauty of following Jesus. Like the daffodils which, against all odds, burst bright and yellow against a dreary backdrop of spring, this is the perfect work of Jesus' love for you.

Let me offer you a personal example. As a young mother with two small children, I was often angry when my husband had to work late. He isn't a workaholic, but sometimes he couldn't help but have a late evening completing his assigned tasks. When he finally arrived home I would give him the silent treatment, making sure he understood my anger by my cold shoulder. But I began to realize this was helping no one, and especially not myself as my anger grew like a weed, choking out the joy.

So I decided to use those extra hours talking with Jesus. I would share my frustration and ask for strength in my parenting. I looked for happy moments playing with my small children, and prayed for a patient, loving heart when my husband returned. Slowly, I changed. I became less of an angry wife when my husband walked in the door, and more joyful, happy, patient, and kind in my communication. This is the beauty of following Jesus. It changes us.

Like me, do you find yourself in need of the one who loves like no other? The one whose love changes you for the better? Now understand, following Jesus is not the easy life, ridding you of all difficulties; no matter our journey, the pain of life never fails to sting. However, following Jesus is a deeply fulfilling and rich life in the middle of both the beautiful and the broken.

God's Word tells us that we are needy, and he is limitless. We are broken, and he is the healer. We are deficient, and he is perfect. When we come to fully realize our insufficiency, we can truly see he is what we need.

If I'm honest, I'm still deeply needy and broken and deficient, and there is not a day that passes where I do not reach out asking Jesus to help me. But after years of following Jesus I am less broken and less deficient; now I am more whole, stronger, and at peace with myself and others. Jesus' love has cocooned me and changed me from who I was into who he created me to be; it is a process not a potion.

Dear one, is there something holding you back from following Jesus? Please journal your thoughts below.

After that, grab your Bible and look up John 10:10. No worries if you don't have a Bible; just do a quick google search to find it. Consider the life Jesus is freely offering you.

A checklist does not define those who follow Jesus, nor does obedience to a list of rules. Instead, following Jesus cultivates within your heart a blossoming garden, one full of flourishing in a fruitful relationship. A garden tucked away in your soul which even the most fierce of storms cannot destroy.

Here are some comforting realities about what it means to follow Jesus, straight from the Bible:

- "Every person who has walked this earth needs Jesus; he loves us exactly where we are and died for us when we didn't even know he cared. But God showed his great love for us by sending Christ to die for us while we were still sinners" (Romans 5:8, NLT).

- "For he has rescued us from the kingdom of darkness and transferred us into the Kingdom of his dear Son, who purchased our freedom and forgave our sins" (Colossians 1:13-14, NLT).

- "I pray that God, the source of hope, will fill you completely with joy and peace because you trust in him. Then you will overflow with confident hope through the power of the Holy Spirit" (Romans 15:13, NLT).

If you have never said, "Jesus, I want to follow you," then let me invite you to pray these words with me. "Jesus, you alone are the way, the truth, and the life. I believe you died for my sins so I can live. I trust you and I will follow you all the days of my life."

Welcome to new life, dear one! As followers of Jesus, we want to soak up as much sunlight as possible so we can flourish. There are so many ways you can do this, but let me lay out a few steps for you:

- Spend time reading or listening to God's Word. Set a time of the day, and let this habit become a rhythm in your daily life. The timing of this will ebb and flow with different seasons of life, so be mindful that this is a rhythm, not a rule.

- There are many wonderful Bible studies you can purchase, or you can read a few chapters of the Bible every day. I recommend you begin with the book of John, then move to Ephesians. John will teach you so much about Jesus, and Ephesians will teach you so much about Jesus in you. This is a beautiful combination.

What is one step you can take to begin your journey of faith?

BATTERED FAITH

One summer afternoon cloaked in sunshine, my friend and I walked under a brilliant sky that betrayed her dark emotions. In deep grief she turned to me and asked me, "Will I ever trust God again?" You see, together we had prayed and believed God for a pertinent need, only to have her life crumble around her. I scoured my heart for a wise response and came up empty.

Looking back, I wish someone would have told me that trust is much more challenging than one originally anticipates. I wish someone would have said, "Heather, trust will take more courage than you ever imagine." And most importantly, I wish someone would have reassured me that even shaky trust is still trust, like a child learning to walk.

In this season of life, the Psalms became dear to me. The psalmists who spoke in gut-wrenching honesty about their feelings towards God resonated with me. The Psalms they wrote that expressed these emotions are called laments. A lament is defined as a "passionate expression of grief or sorrow." We see them throughout scripture, as they were a way for God's people to bring their complaints before his throne.

There is no formula to a lament, no right or wrong answers. But a general outline looks like this:

- Expression of complaints, grievances, and pain
- Request for God to act
- Statement of surrender and trust because of who God is

Why don't you use the outline above and take some time to write a lament? (If you would like some examples, you can find laments in Psalm 3, 7, 13, 30, 88, 79, 137.)

Lamenting is one way to walk towards healing. Another way, especially when our faith feels feeble, is to swim back upstream and find the ocean where our faith began. We see this evident in Naomi's story found in the book of Ruth, which begins as one big detour of disappointment. Why don't you take time now to read the beginning of Naomi's story in Ruth 1:1-22.

In reading this story, we see that due to a famine, Naomi, her husband, and their two sons, left Bethlehem and moved to the country of Moab. But Naomi's husband died, leaving her alone with her sons. Then, after her two sons married, her sons also died. In lament, Naomi returned to Bethlehem with her foreign daughter-in-law, telling the people of her town, "Do not call me Naomi; call me Mara (meaning bitter), for the Almighty has dealt very bitterly with me. I went away full, and the Lord has brought me back empty."

Yet Naomi did an interesting thing. She trusted Boaz, her family's kinsman redeemer, and placed her future in his hands. The roles of a kinsman redeemer are laid out in the Levitical Law (Leviticus 25). In summary, a kinsman redeemer is a family relative who helps a weaker relative in need, or who willingly pays off the debts of a relative—essentially buying back what was lost due to the debt. From the time Naomi returned to Bethlehem, she knew that Boaz was their close relative and a "worthy man," and Naomi trusted Boaz would uphold the law.

Initially, Naomi sent her daughter-in-law, Ruth, to glean in his fields. Then, after seeing how Boaz protected and provided for Ruth in the fields, Naomi sent Ruth to lay at Boaz's feet while he slept.

At the time, this was seen as a request for him to be their redeemer.

But Boaz didn't stop at fulfilling the requirements of the law, he exceeded them. Boaz bought Naomi's family land, fulfilling the law, but then he also married Ruth and had a child with her so Naomi's family line would continue. As Naomi cradled her new grandson, her friends called out a tune far different from Naomi's words that she said upon her return. They said, "Blessed be the Lord, who has not left you this day without a redeemer. He shall be to you a restorer of life and nourisher of your old age."

Naomi, despite her bitterness and despondency, knew her redeemer, and placed her trust in his capable hands. And Boaz was faithful. If this story feels familiar, it should, because Jesus, our Redeemer, repeated this story in our spiritual lives. He is the one who paid our debt of sin by his death on the cross and now calls us his beautiful bride, the ones whom he deeply loves (Isaiah 54:4-8; Revelation 19:7-9).

Like Naomi demonstrated, focusing on the character of God doesn't remove us from this painful world, but it gives us safe harbor through it. So when your life hits a detour filled with disappointment, swim back upstream to the ocean of God's strong character, and saturate yourself in the truth of who God is. He is truly worthy of our trust!

Here are four steps you can take right now:

- Let's see how God defines his character. Look up the verses listed below and note what you learn about God.
    -Psalm 46
    -Psalm 96
    -Ephesians 1:3-10
    -1 John 4:7-21
- Repeat these to yourself often!
- Declare your surrender at the end of your honest lament.
- Surround yourself with people who will speak truth and hope into your life, like Ruth and Naomi did for each other.

What did you learn about God's character after reviewing the listed verses? Consider writing a prayer of lament in the space provided below.

BUILDING FAITH

Sister, I picture you holding this little book and coming to this last page, a page designed to build and encourage your faith. But what does one say to someone who, by the power of God, has already lived as a mighty warrior? You, who have taken the sword of the Spirit and wielded it with power and precision. What does one say to those already walking in truth and life?

I start by saying what I say to my children after every single one of their sporting events: I love watching you play! In the same way, I imagine Jesus smiling upon you with pure joy and thinking, "I love watching you." I don't think he analyzes your every mistake, nor revisits your slip ups and failures. Rather, he is over the moon about you!

Just as a buttercup tilts its face toward the sun, we thrive under the loving warmth of Jesus. Revelations 2 is a clear picture of his priority for the saints who endure. Here, the word of the Lord came to the church in Ephesus, "I know your works, your toil and your patient endurance ... I know you are enduring patiently and bearing up for my name's sake, and you have patiently suffered for me without quitting."

But according to Revelation 2:4, "But I have this complaint against you. You don't love me or each other as you did at first!"

Where had the church in Ephesus missed the mark?

During my younger years, I ran a few half marathons. Usually I got bamboozled into it by a few friends, and then I was committed. The honest truth is that I did not love running. But I spent the hours necessary for training because it was a free and healthy workout, one where I could buckle my kids into a stroller.

See the correlation? I was like the church in Ephesus, I had everything but love. So unfortunately, my running hasn't outlasted my kids aging out of the jogging stroller. But what if I loved running? I know a few crazy ladies who do! They keep running. And running. And running.

Let me offer you a gentle nudge, something I'm asking myself even as I write these words. In a spiritual sense, where is your first love? Have you, like the church in Ephesus, toiled and patiently endured, but lost this love? Have you noticed any changes in priorities during the years of your maturing faith?

Take a few moments and talk with God about how you loved him, and what, if anything, has changed?

Think back to your younger relationship with Jesus. Maybe it was in college, or as a high school teen, or young adult. How might you maintain the "love you had at first?"

When we love someone, whether it's the love of a friend or the love of a spouse, spending time with that person becomes a priority. So it is with Jesus. To continue deepening our relationship with Jesus, we must continue to spend time with him. When I look back on my life, my closest friends are the ones I talked to most often.

Here are some suggestions to get you started:

- Find a local church where you can be involved. Spend time serving in the church and connecting with the other members.
- If your church does not offer a women's Bible study, connect with one in your local area. Bible Study Fellowship, Precepts, and Community Bible Studies are all wonderful options.
- Develop rhythms of prayer. These rhythms will change throughout our different seasons of life. For example, when my children were little, I used their naptime to write and pray in my journal; now that my children are all in school, I spend my time walking the dog or cleaning the dishes talking with God. Once you have begun the habit of talking with Jesus throughout your day, you will never go back.

Thankfully, in Jesus, nothing is wasted. Nothing is lost. Not even the years of toil and patient endurance.

But let me leave you with this charge: God is love, and whoever abides in love abides in God, and God abides in him. So beloved, let us love one another, for love is from God, and, first and foremost, let us love the Lord our God with all our heart and with all our soul and with all our mind.

What one or two things will you commit to doing to help build your faith?

"So, you have sorrow now, but I will see you again; then you will rejoice, and no one can rob you of that joy."

—John 16:22 (NLT)

ABOUT THE AUTHOR

Darlene Brock has always been one to push the limits of what's possible. Determined to figure out life on her own terms, she left home at 18 and quit her first job as a receptionist at a prestigious law firm to live in a Christian commune. After a brief stint running a summer camp and conference center, Darlene spent more than 20 years in the music business with her husband, Dan, producing award-winning music videos, managing music groups, promoting concerts, and serving as COO of ForeFront Records.

Over the course of her career, Darlene realized there were two tenets that helped her tackle the trials and triumphs life threw her way: grit and grace. This realization led her and Dan to launch The Grit and Grace Project, a nonprofit, faith-based media organization whose mission is to remind all women that true beauty is found in their strength.

It was through her work as co-founder and president of The Grit and Grace Project and her own motherhood journey that Darlene recognized the need for honest, unfiltered, and encouraging advice for moms.

Inspired to arm other mothers with the tools needed to raise confident and capable girls, Darlene wrote her first book, *Raising Great Girls*, which details the various roles and responsibilities a mom will take on as she sets her daughter on the path to success.

Darlene has been featured on *Fox & Friends, Focus on the Family, Keep the Faith, The Todd Starnes Show, Family Life Today* and multiple ABC, CBS, NBC and FOX affiliates. She has been a featured columnist for CNN and written for numerous family magazines and websites including *Home Life* magazine and *AUTHENTIC* magazine. She's also a commonly requested podcast guest, appearing in shows such as *Jesus Calling, Stronger in the Difficult Places, Coffee and Kettlebells, 5 Minute Mom, Modern Motherhood, MARKED* by LifeWay Women, and *Rebel Parenting*.

Darlene's life as an author, mother, businesswoman, wife, and creative producer continues to underscore the truth behind The Grit and Grace Project's motto: that life challenges should neither defeat nor define you. And, just so you know, she wears the tool belt in her family.

Instagram: https://www.instagram.com/darlenebrock7/

Facebook : https://www.facebook.com/DarleneBrockAuthor

Twitter: https://twitter.com/DarleneBrock7

LinkedIn: https://www.linkedin.com/in/darlene-brock-21833925/

Raising Great Girls: https://amzn.to/3N2jPF2

www.gritandgracelife.com

www.darlenebrock.com

"Life will be brighter than noonday, and darkness will become like morning. You will be secure, because there is hope."

—Job 11:17-18a

RESOURCES

Use this QR code to access a free printable companion journal, additional books related to the topic, and more.

Below are additional books in the Smart Living series.

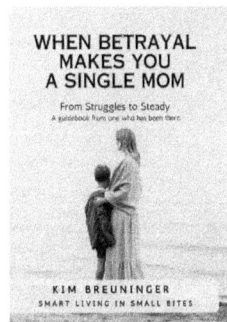

WHEN SUICIDE TOUCHES YOUR LIFE
From Hurt to Healing
A guidebook from one who has been there
DARLENE BROCK
SMART LIVING IN SMALL BITES

WHEN YOUR PAST ABUSE STILL HURTS
From Broken to Restored
A guidebook from one who has been there
ALLISON MCCORMICK
SMART LIVING IN SMALL BITES

WHEN ANXIETY WON'T LET GO
From Panic to Peace
A guidebook from one who has been there
CAROLINE BEIDLER, MSW
SMART LIVING IN SMALL BITES

WHEN MARRIAGE IS HARD
From Conflict to Connection
A guidebook from one who has been there
JULIE BENDER
SMART LIVING IN SMALL BITES

WHEN DATING AGAIN FEELS SCARY
From Fearful to Courageous
A guidebook from one who has been there
MARLYS JOHNSON LAWRY
SMART LIVING IN SMALL BITES

WHEN BETRAYAL MAKES YOU A SINGLE MOM
From Struggles to Steady
A guidebook from one who has been there
KIM BREUNINGER
SMART LIVING IN SMALL BITES

Coming Soon

Other Books

At *Grit and Grace Life*, we strive to bring you great articles every day. Over the years, we've had the honor of sharing practical tips and helpful wisdom with our readers. We couldn't do this without our team of talented writers. Like you, these women are learning to navigate the ups and downs of life with grit and grace.

What you may not know is that many of our writers have dug a bit deeper and written books that can help you (or someone you love) on your journey. Are you ready to change your life?

Use this QR code to access a list of books written by *Grit and Grace Life* writers.

ABOUT GRIT AND GRACE LIFE

Grit and Grace Life is a place for strong women and those who want to be. As a community of women, we have come together to share the life lessons we have learned and the wisdom we have gained. Whether it's through books, videos, social media, podcasts, or on our website, our goal in everything we do is to help women navigate this challenging and wonderful life.

We tackle all things women face, whether big or small, knowing that as we do, we will find strength. We are a collective from every age and every stage of life, here to pass on our stories and the answers we've found through the joys and challenges of our lives. Our driving desire is to provide insights, real-life solutions, hope, and encouragement to all who walk alongside us.

Faith is paramount to who we are and what we do. We have been gently guided in our lives by a God who loves us faithfully and completely. It is in him we find hope and healing. We believe you will, too.

Through all we do at Grit and Grace Life, our prayer is that you would embrace grit and grace as the strongholds of your life, just as we have. And, please, remember this: Grit determines that life challenges won't defeat or define us. Grace gives kindness to ourselves and others, even when it's hard.

www.gritandgracelife.com

The *Smart Living with Grit and Grace* podcast can be heard at:
https://smartlivingwithgritandgrace.org/podcast

Follow us on social media:
https://www.facebook.com/ThisGritandGraceLife
https://www.instagram.com/thisgritandgracelife/
https://www.youtube.com/watch?v=mS4O3YC2Ejw

www.ingramcontent.com/pod-product-compliance
Lightning Source LLC
Chambersburg PA
CBHW071623040426
42452CB00009B/1459